JUST WHAT IS THE CHRISTIAN LIFE ABOUT ANYWAY

JUST WHAT IS THE CHRISTIAN LIFE ABOUT ANYWAY

R. Jason Ray

TATE PUBLISHING
AND ENTERPRISES, LLC

The opinions expressed by the author are not necessarily those of Tate Publishing, LLC.

Published by Tate Publishing & Enterprises, LLC
127 E. Trade Center Terrace | Mustang, Oklahoma 73064 USA
1.888.361.9473 | www.tatepublishing.com

Tate Publishing is committed to excellence in the publishing industry. The company reflects the philosophy established by the founders, based on Psalm 68:11,
"The Lord gave the word and great was the company of those who published it."

Book design copyright © 2014 by Tate Publishing, LLC. All rights reserved.
Cover design by Erin DeMoss
Interior design by Christina Hicks

Published in the United States of America

ISBN: 978-1-63268-299-4
1. Religion / Christian Life / General
2. Religion / Biblical Meditations / General
14.10.29

Table of Contents

Introduction

When I became a believer, the next logical step was to follow, to lead the good Christian life. But I had to find out what this really meant. I've heard some people say that the Christian life is about being good; others say it's about charity works; others say witnessing, and still others (most actually) simply don't know. Obviously I couldn't just follow what other people told me was the good Christian life. I had to consult the source—the Bible—and find the answers and the reasons for the answers for myself. The most obvious concept, the one that jumped out at me first, is that Christ is the center of Christianity. *Everything* revolves around Him. That's why we named our religion after Him. The next concept is that our religion should be modeled on the gospel. After all, that is what separates us from other religions. I decided that I was going to have to write down all my questions and read the Bible for myself and write down what I came across as I read in order to understand what the Christian life is all about. This is as basic as I can get it.

First, nail down your salvation. You cannot go any farther until you have this right. Salvation is purely through faith; it has nothing to do with works at all. But Jesus died to establish a relationship between you and God. This relationship is important, and this relationship is the reason for good works.

Salvation is achieved simply through believing that Jesus died to pay the penalty for your sins. The gospel in a nutshell: If you believe that Jesus's death pays the penalty for your sins, then you are saved no matter what you do, and if you do not believe, then you cannot be saved no matter what you do, but you should *want* to do right because you know that is what God wants, and you should want to try to please a God who loves you so much.

But attaining salvation is not the ultimate end of Christianity. It is merely the beginning and foundation. Once you're saved, the Christian life is about reflecting the gospel in everything you do. People should see the gospel in every aspect of your lives. The main ways are in the following areas:

Love and charity: God loves us so much that He has given us our salvation, which we could never attain by our own works and didn't deserve and still don't deserve. When you believe this, you must love and give for others just as your heavenly Father has done for you and show them the love that God has for them. How can you know that God loved and gave so much for you even though you never deserved it and yet you won't love and give for others? When you know how much God loves and gives for people, how can you not love and give for them also? How can you not love and give for someone God has loved and given so much for?

Forgiveness: God has forgiven you of all your sin and will keep forgiving you as you continue to sin, so how can you not show this forgiveness to others, even as they continue to sin against you? Since we are guilty but forgiven and will always be guilty but will always be forgiven, we must always forgive the guilt of others.

Witness: God gives salvation to all who believe. But they can't believe if you don't tell them. Since salvation is not about what you have done for God but what He has done for you and since salvation is the most important part of anyone's spiritual life, then the most important part of anyone's spiritual life is that they hear the gospel. The most important thing you can do for God is to tell people the gospel. God has given you the one thing you cannot attain for yourself: salvation. He has also given you the privilege and responsibility to pass it on to others.

Good works: Even though we are set free from the law, we should still study, preach, and try to obey it—even though we know we can never live up to it. The reason for this is that the law exists to remind us our unworthiness before God and our need for a Savior. Our good works is simply our way of showing our love for God. But we cannot be saved if we do not first admit our sin, and once we admit our sin, we must then admit that we should do better. Also we cannot win souls to Jesus if we cannot convince them of their sin problem. Preaching about the law will also keep us from taking Christ for granted. But we must remember that good works has nothing to do with salvation. There are some people who are blatant sinners but are saved, and there are some who seem to never sin but aren't saved. Good works is always requested but never required. This is because we are not capable of living the righteous life that is required to attain salvation through works. But we must learn to see sin as an evil that needs to be controlled instead of some small thing that we don't need to worry about. We should want to be righteous just because we know that is what God likes.

There are lots of people who say that since Jesus paid for all our sins, then righteousness is not as important as loving, giving, and witnessing. But how can we recognize our sinfulness and our need for a Savior and have no desire to change? How can we know that our sin separates us from God and still not want to do right? How can we understand God's repulsion at our sin and yet we continue in it? But our main focus is to provide for the poor as God has provided for us and tell lost souls how we found salvation and how they can find it too. The goal of our good works is not to attain or even maintain salvation. It is simply because we want to be what God wants us to be. It also doesn't all happen at once. It takes a lifetime to master.

The New Testament clearly teaches that we are free from the law, that we can basically get away with anything and still be saved, but how can we be happy with our sin if we know God doesn't like it? That is why it calls for us to volunteer to be holy. Galatians 5:13 says, "For you are called to freedom, brothers; only don't use this freedom as an opportunity for the flesh, but to serve one another through love." This means that through Christ, we are set free from the bondage to the law and given a new mission of love that reflects the gospel, but love for God should make us want to obey His law.

The Christian life is about taking up your cross, about considering what the cross means and reflecting it to those around you. The ultimate goal of the Christian life is to become a fisher of men. After all, this is the first and last thing Jesus told His disciples. Everything we do should be to lead us toward this goal. That is why everything we do should reflect the gospel.

I certainly don't want you to read this book thinking I've got it all figured out. I don't. I just want to show you some of the things I've seen so you can see them clearly as you read your Bible. Think of this book as merely a starting point that gives you things to look for as you read your Bible. Also don't think I'm a saint. I still struggle to live up to this simple formula myself. Everyone does.

Salvation

The central concept of Christianity is salvation through faith alone. Everything you do in the Christian life will be based on it. Getting saved is not all that the Christian life is about- it is only the foundation. There are other things that you will focus on once you're saved but since salvation is the base, you need to nail it down first.

If you believe that Jesus's death pays for your sins, then you are saved. That's it. Even future sins are paid for because God knew we would still sin. He even knew some people would take advantage of it. Although God wants us to be holy, He still forgives those who take advantage of His forgiveness. That's the wonder of God's forgiveness! Also, those who try to be righteous cannot look down on those who don't because the truth is that they are still no better. The best we can do is nothing but filthy rags in God's eyes. God cannot punish us for sin that has already been paid for, so if Jesus paid the penalty for our sins, then we have nothing to worry about. Jesus is all we need. Salvation is not through works or even "faith and works." It is purely through our faith that Jesus's death pays for all our sins. Works and baptism have nothing to do with salvation. They are *products of* our salvation, as I will explain later in the book. The reason God made salvation through faith alone is that man is not capable of the kind of righteousness that is required to achieve salvation through works. This is the main point of the Old Testament since all you see as you read it is that the people of God always backslide.

In order to achieve salvation through works, we would have to be perfect. No one can ever even come close. It's the same way with "faith and works" because man will always sin and therefore lose his salvation. Some people try to defend a "faith and works" salvation by saying that salvation is through works but our faith in Jesus pays for the times we slip up. What they don't realize is that this is really a good defense for a faith-alone salvation because in order to defend their position, they must admit that they cannot achieve salvation without Jesus. They must admit that they are sinners and that Jesus paid for their sins. They must admit that the only reason they are saved is because of their faith that Jesus paid for their sins, which is salvation through faith alone. This is why Jesus either means everything or He means nothing. There is no "faith and works" salvation because this system implies that Jesus died for your sins but that His death doesn't mean anything because you still have to be perfect in order to maintain salvation. So it's obvious that "faith and works" is an oxymoron. To believe in faith and works is to believe that your works are at least equal with Christ's death and to believe that His death is insufficient. That is why people who believe in "faith and works" are not saved. They do not truly believe that Jesus's death can pay for all their sins. Also, they almost always put more faith in their works than in their faith. To believe in Christ alone is to believe that He is enough and that you cannot be anything. The entire New Testament teaches that salvation is purely through faith. Our good works are simply out of love.

God is so holy that He cannot associate with sin. Sin must be paid for somehow, and God has graciously allowed substitution in the sacrifice system that is intermingled with the Old Testament law. But even Old Testament sacrifice was only meant to point the way forward to God's provision of the ultimate sacrifice. No man can offer enough sacrifice on his own to pay for all his sins. His unpaid sins still far outweigh his paid sins, and so he must pay the price with his soul. By this reckoning, no man can ever be spared from eternity in hell. Thus, the devil would win. But God loves us so much that He offered to win the battle for us. He gave us Jesus to be an infinite sacrifice for us so that by faith (which is the only thing man is capable of getting right) we may be made pure. This means that even when we still sin, Jesus's death still pays for it. That's the wonder of God's grace, that He continues to forgive even though He knows you will continue to sin! All our sins are paid for! We don't have any unpaid sin and therefore cannot be sent to hell. Fighting the battle for ourselves, we will always lose, but when God fights for us, we always win! The devil is defeated! God has won for us!

Since the concept of salvation through faith alone is all that separates Christianity from other religions and is the central concept of our religion, we must study and accept this concept. Without this concept, Jesus means nothing to us. He is merely a prophet or teacher. But even if we only see Jesus as a prophet or teacher, we must study and understand

His teachings since we call Him a teacher. Since Jesus clearly taught so many times that He is our salvation, then to see Jesus as a prophet or teacher and miss the concept of Him being our Savior is to miss the central point of His teachings, which is to say that the teacher taught us nothing or that we missed His point or simply didn't pay attention. Since Jesus Himself clearly taught that He is our only way to heaven, it is impossible to see Him as a prophet or teacher without also accepting Him as our Savior; so if we study Jesus's teachings, we must accept that He is our only way to heaven. We must also look at the lives of the disciples. When Jesus was crucified, they were ready to go back to being fishermen, hoping they could disappear so that no one would recognize them as followers of Jesus. But after Jesus's resurrection, they changed even to the point that they went all over the world telling people that Jesus paid for their sins. They even went to their deaths proclaiming the message of salvation through faith alone. If Jesus did not teach that He is the only way to heaven and did not rise from the dead, then the disciples would not have taught that Jesus died for our sins and was raised from the dead. They would have gone back to being fishermen, their lives never would have changed, they probably would have gone back to Judaism or Paganism, and we would have never heard of Jesus.

Next, we should look at the most famous conversion story in the New Testament: Paul's. Paul didn't just hear the gospel and believe. He had a divine encounter with Jesus on the road to Damascus. This divine encounter would not have happened if it would have led to false doctrine (since God knew what the outcome would be and would not have given Paul his conversion experience and sent him to people who would share the gospel if God did not want salvation by faith alone to be taught). Therefore we must assume that Paul's doctrine was sound, and since he taught that Jesus is our Savior and our only way to heaven, we must accept this teaching as true.

Finally, we must study the teachings of the New Testament. It seems that all the passages of the New Testament deal with the concept of salvation through faith alone or with how to live our lives based on the gospel. The gospel is the string that holds the entire New Testament together. Without the gospel, the whole New Testament would fall apart. All of the books of the New Testament teach that salvation is by faith alone and has nothing to do with works. Our works are simply out of love.

I do have a warning, though. It is that we must have true faith in order to be saved. Unfortunately, many people call themselves Christians, but they haven't really stopped to ask themselves what they really believe. They just go to church simply because they think that's what they are supposed to do, or maybe they think salvation has something to do with how often they go to church. They are just going through the motions. They haven't personally accepted that Jesus died to pay the penalty for their sins so they can go to heaven. Or maybe they are still trying to work their way to heaven in a "faith and works" theology. They are spiritually dead and are not saved because their faith in Jesus's death atoning for their sins is really nonexistent. It's not real and personal to them. We must assess our faith and be sure it is real. We must *truly* believe. Going along with the motions will not save us. Accepting the beliefs of others will not save us. We have to come to the point in our lives where we make it personal for ourselves. Each of us has to be able to say, "I'm going to heaven because Jesus died for my sins," and believe it with certainty. We cannot say, "I'm going to heaven because Jesus died for my sins and I am trying to do the best I can."

So how does good works into the picture of Christianity? It comes because of your salvation. It happens *after* salvation. You are saved simply by acknowledging your sin and having faith in Jesus's atoning death. But *then* you must ask yourself the question, "Do I want to serve myself and sin, or do I want to serve God?" Once saved always saved, even for a carnal Christian, but the carnal Christian should be struggling to live with his sin because he knows he is wrong. Once saved always saved, but how can you love sin and God at the same time?

Depart from Me

Jesus says

> Not everyone who says to me "Lord, Lord!" will enter the kingdom of heaven, but [only] the one who does the will of my Father in heaven. On that day many will say to Me, "Lord, Lord, didn't we prophesy in your name, drive out demons in your name, and do many miracles in your name?" Then I will announce to them, "I never knew you! Depart from Me, you lawbreakers!"

Matthew 7:21-23

What does He mean? Does He mean that those who don't live perfectly righteous lives will not go to heaven even if they know Jesus as Lord and Savior? No. The reason is that no one is able to live that life. Also, if this is what He meant, then His death would not have accomplished anything. Also, look at verse 22. People who cast out demons, prophesied, and worked miracles could not enter heaven. Who can be better than that? I know I can't! So what does it really mean? Look at verse 21: "Only the one who does the will of My Father in heaven." Now look at John 6:28-29: "'What can we do to perform the works of God?' they asked. Jesus replied, 'This is the work of God: that you believe in the One He has sent.'" That's the key! Notice in Matthew 7:23 that the reason Jesus tells the people to depart from Him is that He never knew them. But I must warn you it's not so easy to know Jesus. Believing that Jesus was real, was the Son of God, that He was born of a virgin, lived a sinless life, worked miracles, died and rose again after three days will do nothing for you. You must believe in Him as Savior, that His death pays for all your sins and gives you a place in heaven. That's the meaning of the passage. Too many of us call ourselves Christians but don't really believe or don't fully grasp the concept of Jesus's death paying for our sins. We kind of just go along with the flow. The will of God is that you believe that Jesus's death pays for your sins and that your faith is all you need to go to heaven. You do not have to be perfect after your salvation (but it's still good to try to be good) because your sins have already been paid for. Those who do not believe this are not truly saved because they have not fully grasped the concept of their inability to be perfect or of Jesus's death paying for their sins. They don't really believe that Jesus paid for *all* their sins. In the Old Testament, when someone offered a sacrifice, their guilt was transferred to the animal. But the Old Testament sacrifice was only meant to point the way to God's provision of the ultimate sacrifice. Jesus is our sacrifice, and He is more than adequate to pay for all our sins! You do not know Jesus until you know Him as your Savior. Does this mean that all who accept Jesus as their personal Savior will go to heaven no matter what they do? Jesus says:

> Because of this, I tell you, people will be forgiven every sin and blasphemy, but the blasphemy against the spirit will not be forgiven. Whoever speaks a word against the Son of Man, it will be forgiven Him, but whoever speaks against the Holy Spirit, it will not be forgiven Him, either in this age or the age to come.
>
> Matthew 12:31-32

This means that for all those who know Jesus as Savior, their sins are forgiven. For all who know Jesus as Savior, the only way they can lose their salvation is by blasphemy.

Read John 6:60-66, Matthew 13:24-30, and Matthew 13:36-43. In these passages, Jesus shows His disciples that not everyone who appears to be His disciple really is one. The difference is in three areas. The first is in understanding that attaining heaven is not about how good you've been but about accepting Jesus. The second is in knowing Jesus as Savior—not just as the Son of God, born of a virgin, who did miracles and was raised from the dead but as Savior. The third is in true faith. There are many people who go to church every week but don't have true faith. Your faith must be real. You are not saved if you are just going through the motions.

Read Matthew 25:31-46. Why does Jesus say that charity is what separates true believers from unbelievers? It's because of what the gospel means. It means that God loves everybody, that He has given us more than we could ever attain by ourselves, and that He has forgiven us. Therefore, those who believe the gospel must reflect this belief through charity. If you believe that God loves someone and has given His Son for them, how can you not love them and give them something you have in order to tell them that Jesus died for their sins?

In Mark 8:34, what does it mean when Jesus says, "If anyone wants to follow Me, he must deny himself, take up his cross, and follow Me"? People say that it means you must die to sin, that you must be willing to die, and that you must be willing to suffer. I think it may mean all of these, but the way I like to see it is meaning that a true follower of Christ must base all his actions on the cross, on the gospel. It means we must think about what the cross means and live it out. Remember what the cross means. It means that God loves everybody, even the vilest sinners. It means that sin is a terrible thing that we need to try to control. It means that God gave us something that was precious to Him: His Son. It means that God has forgiven us and will keep on forgiving us no matter how badly we sin. And it means that God has given us the salvation we do not deserve and the authority to give it to others. It also means that we are to volunteer to endure the ridicule, hate, and persecution from nonbelievers that Jesus volunteered to endure on the cross. This means that as true followers of Christ, our focus is on showing love, charity, and forgiveness (to even the worst of people even if they don't deserve it), and helping others to find the salvation that God has given us and to not be ashamed to do it. That's what it means to base our actions on the gospel. That's what it means to take up our cross. That's what it means to be Christian.

General Reasons for Christian Righteousness

Ever since New Testament times, people have been asking, "If Jesus paid for all my sins, then why do I need to be good?" Paul addressed this in many of his writings. He acknowledges that Christians can basically get away with anything and still be saved but encourages them to do right because God has a better plan for their lives. In 1 Corinthians 10:23, he puts it as simple as he can: "'Everything is permissible,' but not everything is helpful. 'Everything is permissible,' but not everything builds up." Here he acknowledges that we are set free from the law but says that the reason we should try to be righteous is to help others and to build ourselves up. Trying to be righteous is something that each Christian must decide for himself. We are clearly set free from having to uphold the law, but is there any reason why we should try to uphold it anyway? We all know that no one can be perfect, that the best we can do is nothing but filthy rags in

God's eyes. The reason for the illustration of filthy rags is that rags are used to wipe away dirt. If the rags are used to wipe away dirt, then they get dirt on them. This means that when God looks at our attempts at righteousness that we do in order to cover our sin, He cannot see our righteousness because our sin is all over it. If good works were required for salvation, not even preachers would make it (Matthew 5:20, Matthew 5:48). If we know we can never be perfect and our sin is already paid for, then why try? I believe that righteousness is something we should focus on a little but should never get in the way of loving, giving, forgiving, studying correct theology, and witnessing. Do not think that you can only love, give, and witness if you are righteous. We should never put any of these off in order to focus on our righteousness. In fact, our righteousness should never get in the way of these. But I will never say not to do good works because there are too many good reasons for it and it's just the right thing to do. Our righteousness is something we do voluntarily despite being set free from the law. We do it simply because we know it's right and are not happy with our sin. Are Christians who don't do good works still saved? Yes! You are saved simply by believing that Jesus's death pays for your sins even if you do not do good works, but what are the reasons a Christian should try to be good?

Just because you can get away with something, does that mean that it is okay to do? No. And just because God will continue to forgive you when you sin, that does not mean that it is okay in His eyes? No. He will always forgive you, but He is still grieved and appalled at your sin. He still wants you to try to be righteous.

In order to be saved, we must first admit that we are sinners and that sin is wrong. Salvation is through faith alone, but you can only have faith in Jesus if you believe that you are a sinner and know that sin is wrong. If you know that you are a sinner and that sin is wrong, then you should have at least some desire to change.

Do you want to be as close to God as possible? Do you want a relationship with Him, not just knowledge of Him? You can't get closer to God by running away from Him. Sin in our lives will make us unable to see God clearly even though we know that as believers in Jesus, we will never be away from God. Our righteousness doesn't come from a desire to attain salvation. It comes from a desire to have a closer fellowship with God. Our life is about living out God's will for us. We cannot do this if we are always sinning. We've got to learn to think more about spiritual thoughts than carnal thoughts, to love God more than we love the world. We've got to learn to focus more on eternal things and less on the temporary.

Do you love God? If you do, then why do you constantly choose to disobey Him? Our primary focus is love, and one of the things we should do is to show love toward God by obeying Him. We should not show hate to Him by rebelling against His authority and disobeying Him. We don't try to be good in order to be blessed by God. We do it in order to bless Him.

God has set you free from the power of sin. God has defeated Satan for you. So why do you keep serving Satan by serving sin? You belong to God. God lives through us because the gospel lives through our new mission that God has given us. God lives in us, and we are His temple because the temple is the place where people go to receive forgiveness of sins and to learn about God. We are the ones who spread the gospel and therefore distribute forgiveness of sins to the world, and we are the ones who understand the mysteries of God. We are the ones He has revealed Himself to, and we are His temple because we reveal Him to others.

God loves us so much that He keeps letting us go astray. Why don't you show Him some love by continually coming back to Him? How often are you going to take advantage of God's forgiveness?

We should be trying to please God, kind of like if your wife isn't mad at you but you bring her flowers anyway. The Holy Spirit living inside us makes us want to obey God even though we know we don't have to in order to maintain salvation. We are set free from the law, but the Holy Spirit inside us makes us always think of God and desire righteousness.

God should be obeyed just because He is God. If you have faith in God, you must have faith that His ways are right. You must have faith that what He has revealed to you is better than your own desires.

This is something I call the four steps to righteousness because of salvation:

1. You have eternal life because you believe that Jesus died for your sins, and

2. You understand that the earth is the blink of an eye and eternity is forever, so

3. You understand that your real citizenship is in heaven, so

4. You understand that you are not of this world, so you should try to live like a citizen of heaven.

Through Christ, God has saved not just our lives but our souls. We owe Him a debt of gratitude, a "life debt." We should want to volunteer to do things for Him. Our keeping of the law is not out of necessity but out of gratitude for His grace.

Romans 8:29 says, "For those He foreknew He also predestined to be conformed to the image of His Son, so that He would be the firstborn among many brothers." This means that as those who follow Christ, our mission is to try to be like Him.

What do you want God to say when you meet Him: "Why did you keep doing what you knew was wrong?" or "Well done, good and faithful servant?" When you meet God and look back on your life, do you want to be proud or ashamed?

Righteousness is not something we have to show in order to maintain our salvation but is something we should want to show anyway. When you come to realize that sin is bad and that it grieves God, you should want to stop. Unfortunately, there will always be some sin. You will never get rid of it all, not in this life anyway. Sin is something that you should want to do away with but will never be able to stop completely. It will be a constant struggle for the rest of your life. You will find that you keep doing what you don't want to do. Your soul wants to please God, but your body wants to please itself. We should want to sin less, but should always remember that we will never be sinless. You will have this internal struggle for the rest of your life. Some people will seem to be able to stop sinning, but others will not. Everybody's different. Just do what you can.

So how is a Christian (especially those of us with strong-holds) supposed to get rid of sin? In the Sermon on the Mount, Jesus taught that sin comes from the heart. This means that the key to righteousness is through changing our hearts. We should not be asking God to give us the strength to resist. Instead, we should be asking Him to renew our minds and our hearts. Read Romans 6:15-23. Notice that Paul says to "offer yourselves." This means that it is voluntary. Also notice verse 17: "obeyed from the heart." This means that the reason for good works is out of love for God. Now look at verse 19. Notice it says "greater and greater." This means that right-eousness doesn't come naturally. It is something that we must work at over a long time in order to be able to do it. It's not easy. Two of the best ways to control sin are by displacement (filling your life with thoughts about God) and accountabil-ity (having friends keep you on track). Now read Romans 6:15-23 and Romans 12:1-2. The key is in the words *greater and greater* and *renewing of your mind*. The only way to be righteous is by constantly focusing on God and staying in His Word. It's not easy. In fact, it's impossible. That's why God gave us Jesus in the first place.

Look at Romans 7:13-25. Paul tells us that he still struggles. Even though he has tried all his life to keep the law, he still cannot. He admits that he keeps slipping up and that there is nothing he can do to stop sinning. He says that there is nothing he can do to change his nature, and this makes him rejoice to have Jesus as his Savior. But even if you choose not to try to be good, you should still feel remorse about your sins and praise God for giving you salvation. Don't let your sinfulness make you think negatively about yourself. You're only human. Just keep praying for that renewing of your mind and heart.

Romans 7:14-25 talks about our sin nature. Paul is saying that even though we are saved and have given our lives to Christ to obey God's commands, we still have a fleshly desire for sin that we cannot control. Our old sin nature does not go away once we are saved. It will always remain. It's like a glass that's under a faucet. On this faucet, instead of having hot and cold, it has a sin side and a God side. The two sides are connected so that the faucet always flows. If you turn one side off, the other comes on full blast. But no one can turn the faucet all the way to the God side. The glass can't take it. It will burst. So there is always some sin. If we cannot turn all the way to God, then how do we get rid of our sin? We don't. That's because to get rid of our sin is to get rid of our own nature. Paul acknowledges this and says that he struggles, that no matter how hard he tries he cannot stop sinning but that he feels bad when he sins. This is what should happen to all Christians. We should recognize sin's hold on us and realize that we will never get rid of it, but at the same time, we should feel bad about sinning willfully. Paul, at the end of the passage, asks what he can do about his sin nature. His answer is "not much." Then he says that the only thing he can do is to thank God that Jesus has paid his debt for him. I see verses like Matthew 5:48, "be ye therefore perfect as your heavenly Father is perfect," and Matthew 5:20, "Unless your righteousness surpasses that of the scribes and Pharisees you will never enter the kingdom of heaven," and I see that Jesus is not saying we have to be good in order to get to heaven. He is saying that we cannot be good enough, we cannot be perfect, and we cannot be more righteous than the most righteous men on earth. Jesus is saying that the reason He came is to show us our need for a Savior and to pay our debt for us, and Paul is saying he is glad Jesus has come! The reason our sin nature does not change when we get saved is that God wants us to always remember that we are nothing but vile sinners in His eyes and that the best we can do is nothing but filthy rags in His eyes and never to take Christ for granted.

None of us will ever be perfectly righteous, so we shouldn't think we are better than anyone else. When people see us sin, we should be able to tell them that we are no better than anyone else, that we are only sinners undeserving of heaven who are saved by God's grace. We are to show them that the wonder of God's grace is that it still saves us even though God knows we will still sin. This is why we must understand that righteousness is only a secondary focus for us since Jesus has already dealt with our sins. We must remember that the mission God has given us is to show His love, charity, forgiveness, and acceptance and to share the gospel because He desires that others come to be saved also.

So do we have to be righteous to maintain our salvation? No. But we should try anyway just because we know it's the right thing to do. Our purpose in righteousness is not to attain or even maintain salvation. We can't do it. That's why Jesus died for us in the first place. Our purpose in righteousness is not to achieve salvation or to glorify ourselves. It's not even to sanctify ourselves. Our purpose in righteousness is simply to glorify God.

Sure, Jesus's death does pay for all our sins and carnal Christians are saved, but that's not all God wants. Being saved is not the end. It is only the beginning. I'm not suggesting faith and works salvation, and I'm not saying that carnal Christians are not truly saved. As long as you believe in Jesus's death paying for your sins, you are saved. Period. That's it. You do not need to worry about your salvation. The only question is, are you serving, loving, worshipping, praising, and pleasing God? *That* is the reason to try to do right. You can't earn salvation, but you should simply do what God wants just because He's God and He deserves it. That is what God has in mind for your life, worshipping Him and thanking Him. One way to thank God for His salvation is to give Him something in return, and the best thing you can give Him is your love and obedience. He's given you the best thing He could (salvation), so why don't you thank Him by giving Him the best thing you can? It's not about what you can get away with. It's about what you can give back and it's about doing right. It's about *volunteering* for God.

Anybody can love, give, forgive, witness, and at least recognize their need to do right, but only a select few can begin to understand how to live a godly life or how to let God live through you. The reason most people can't live a Godly life is that the method for denying sin is not part of our human nature. But this doesn't mean that it is okay to go around sinning just because it is your nature and you don't know how to stop. Sin is still bad. God still doesn't like it even though He has paid for it by giving His son in our place. It's just that the secret to godly living is hidden in the Bible and is not easy to do. But that doesn't mean we should ignore it. Instead, we should be *searching* for it. I keep falling flat on my face or turning away from God, but God still keeps loving and forgiving me. He keeps forgiving me even though He knows I'll just keep falling. If God keeps forgiving me even when my falls are intentional (as they so often are), then I'll keep getting back up and following God! We should continually be *thanking* God for loving and forgiving us! It's like Jeremiah 33:3 says: "Call unto Me and I will show you great and mighty things you do not understand." But that's just the thing. We have to call on Him and ask Him to reveal it to us. We cannot find it on our own, but if we just search the Scriptures, God will reveal it to us and it will blow our minds! If we just ask, He'll just give it to us! Keep searching!

Our Main Focus

As Christians, our main focus is on reflecting the gospel. The gospel is that God loves us, that He has given us His Son, that He has forgiven our sins, and that He continues to forgive our sins. This means that our main focus is on reflecting God's love, His giving and His forgiving, and sharing the gospel. This is why Jesus commanded us to wash one another's feet and to love one another. This is why Jesus told the rich young ruler to sell all he had and give to the poor, and it is why He told the parable of the sheep and the goats in which those who fed the poor, relieved suffering, took in the homeless, clothed the poor, took care of the sick, and visited prisoners were counted among the saved and those who did not do these things were not. Also, the fruit of the Spirit (Galatians 5:22) is love, joy, peace, patience, kindness, goodness, faith, gentleness, and self-control. That is because our main focus is on showing God's love, and all these come from love. These things are our main focus because sharing the gospel is our main goal. As a Christian, your life is not about you; it's about others. We should do all these things out of the love that comes from believing the gospel. Loving, giving, forgiving, and sharing the gospel is our main focus. Why must a Christian concentrate on these things? Well, how can you believe that God loves the world yet you don't love? How can you believe that God gave something that was precious to Him (His Son) for a vile sinner such as yourself yet you won't give to the poor? How can you believe that God has forgiven your sin and continues to forgive you as you continue to sin yet you won't forgive others? This is why Jesus told Peter in Matthew 18:21-22 that we are to forgive "seventy times seven times." We should continue to forgive no matter how many times we are wronged because God forgives us no matter how many times we wrong Him. We should also be careful never to judge anyone. Look at Matthew 7:1-6 and Romans 2:1-5. How can you judge someone when you know that God will not judge them if they believe in Jesus? How can you not tolerate someone when you know that God accepts us just as we are? How can you judge a sinner when you know that you are nothing but a sinner? Also remember, as reflections of the gospel, these things should lead us to sharing the gospel. These are what we are to do at all times and never forsake.

God knows that as humans we will always fall back into sin, so He has chosen to take care of our sin once and for all through Jesus. Loving, giving, and witnessing are our life goals, but righteousness is our secondary goal. It's important, but it should never take precedence over our primary goal of loving, giving, and witnessing. We should only make righteousness our primary goal if we have extra time and energy. But really, if we have extra time and energy, we need to look for more ways to show love, give, or witness—or at least support those who do.

Throughout this book I have emphasized that salvation is by faith alone and that we are still saved even when we are sinful. I don't mean to say that righteousness is not important or is only a small consideration. It's very important because it's what God wants. But do not think that God can't use you if you are not perfect. He is actually in the habit of using imperfect people because that shows His love. Just be sure to love Him back.

Who You Are in Christ

As Christians, first and foremost, our identity is as fishers as men. If salvation is by faith in Christ alone, then we need to make sure that others hear the gospel so they have a chance to be saved. We have the right—actually the responsibility— to take forgiveness of sins to the entire world. Notice that the first time Jesus spoke with each of His disciples, He said He would make them fishers of men. Also notice that the last thing He said to them was to go tell the world the good news of the gospel. If it is the first and last thing Jesus said to His disciples, then it stands to reason that it must be the most important thing. That's because it is the most important thing because people cannot be saved if we don't share the gospel.

First Corinthians 4:1 calls us servants of Christ and managers of God's mysteries. As servants of Christ, we are to reflect the gospel by showing love, charity, forgiveness, and sharing the gospel. As managers of God's mysteries, we should understand why God made the new covenant and find people to give forgiveness of sins to. We should also study things like theology, messianic prophecy, and apologetics so that we can explain these mysteries to others.

Second Corinthians 5:20 says that we are ambassadors for Christ. In politics, the ambassadors are the ones who are sent by the kings to other places to help the others understand the motives and desires of the king. This means that we Christians are sent by God to tell the world that He desires to offer them forgiveness of sins. As ambassadors, we must also reflect Christ and reflect our true citizenship in heaven by putting away our sinful desires and concentrating on the kingdom of heaven and the Word of God.

We are the body of Christ. Jesus's main mission was to seek and save that which was lost. This is a mission that was too big for Him to accomplish on His own because He only had one body. But since He lives through us now by way of the Holy Spirit, we are now the body of Christ. We are the ones who must carry out His mission. We must seek and save that which is lost.

Ephesians 5:8-11 says that we are the light of the world. If we are the light of the world, then we do not stumble around aimlessly in the dark. We know the path we should take because we see clearly. This means that we should be able to walk a path of both righteousness and salvation through faith in Christ and we should be able to show that path to others clearly. We should not stumble over obstacles, and we should be able to guide others around them. Again, it's not easy.

Acceptance

Read Romans 14. Here, eating is merely Paul's example of either choosing to uphold all the law or only parts of it. So this passage is not just about eating. It is about sin in general. Notice verses 3 and 4. Notice that although we should call others back to repentance and service for the Lord, we have no right to judge or criticize them. We are only to remind them that they are accountable to God. But there are some who are not able to live a holy life. But notice that "the Lord is able to make him stand." This means that God will give him a righteousness that is as good as anyone else's! Praise the Lord!

Since the gospel is about God's love, we should reflect love to all around us. Since the gospel is about God's forgiveness, we should continually forgive those around us who sin against us or against God. Since it sets us free from the law, we should not be angry or look down on those who do not try to live a perfect life according to the law. They have that right because they have been set free from the law of sin and death. Those of us who choose to obey the law should remember that our righteousness is voluntary. We must remember that our choice not to sin is a burden that we have put on ourselves and is simply out of our desire to try to be pleasing to God. We must also remember that even as hard as we try, we still fail miserably. We do not have the right to enforce our choice to try to be righteous on others. We should accept them as they are, knowing that they may have a firmer grasp of salvation than we do since they understand that they have been set free from the law. We should accept them in a humble way because we know that we also have pet sins that we don't understand. We should never judge others because we know that God doesn't judge us in our sin. Also, we know that we are nothing but filthy sinners ourselves who do not deserve God's grace, so why should we (sinners) judge other sinners? Don't let righteousness lead you to judging or to falling away from the gospel or to lack of forgiveness, love, acceptance, and charity. Rather, let the gospel lead you to forgiveness, tolerance, love, acceptance, and a correct attitude about repentance and righteousness.

Don't forget that being good is not something you do because you have to or because you want to try to earn God's grace. Only your faith in Jesus's sacrificial death can do that for you. The true reason for being good is simply for love of God and because you know sin is wrong. Also don't forget that some people will struggle with sin for a long time before they make any progress. The only thing you should do is to remind them of their sin. The rest is between them and God. He will convict or judge them. You are not to try to do God's job! God has given us the jobs of loving, giving, forgiving, acceptance, and charity but has left judging and conviction for Himself. He has not given us the right to do His job! Also, your attempts (and failures!) at righteousness should remind you that God does not judge you in your sin because of your faith in Jesus, and they should remind you that you are no better than others and you cannot maintain your own righteousness. It should also remind you that righteousness is a lifelong process that no one will ever be able to master and that Christian growth is just that: growth. Maturity takes a lifetime.

We must remember that we have been set free from the law and given a new mission of love, forgiveness, acceptance, and charity that reflects the gospel. God has set us free from having to worry about sin, and yet we worry about sin more than anything. We sometimes focus so much on righteousness that we forget that God has already taken care of it for us. We must realize that the reason He set us free is to show us our sin. When we try to be holy, we must see our failure, not our success, because our success is only temporary and our failure keeps happening no matter how hard we try to stay holy. We must see our failure, and it should lead us to praise God and be more accepting of others. We must realize that the reason some people don't try to be holy is because they know it is futile. When we try to be holy and see our futility, then we must understand that we are no better than anyone else and they are no worse than us. All who are saved are equal! We must remember that God has set us free from having to uphold the law and given us a new mission. We must not worry too much about what God has already taken care of for us. Instead we should focus on the new mission that He has given us. This new mission is one of love, charity, forgiveness, acceptance, and witnessing that reflects the gospel.

Putting our main focus on our own righteousness does two things. First, it downplays the role of Christ in our salvation by implying that Christ's death wasn't enough. Second, it increases our own role in salvation by implying that we can be good enough for God. It is unfortunate that God has set us free from the law and given us a new mission of loving, giving, accepting, and witnessing, but most of us forget that and focus so much on our own righteousness that we think we cannot love, give, and witness because we think we are unworthy. Shame on us! The reason our focus is not inward is because we need to go out into the world in order to win the people who do not go to church. The more we focus inward, the less we focus outward. That is one reason why we are set free from the Law. Also remember that when a person becomes a Christian, they may not be good right away. They may take years to come to that point. Some also backslide into a life away from God after many years of walking with Him. We should not judge them; we should lovingly invite them back. Remember that the reason God sent Jesus in the first place is because man cannot be righteous and has proven to be a backslider. The Bible talks a lot about fruit, saying that fruit that is picked too early does not taste good, but fruit that is allowed to ripen on the vine is the best there is. It takes time. Also remember that fruit usually doesn't fall too far from the tree.

Those of us who choose to uphold the law sometimes drive away those who don't. Sometimes it even goes so far as to make the person reject Christ. There are a lot of people who we come across who are not ready to give up the sinful way they live but will accept that Jesus died for their sins. We know that if they just accept Jesus they will be saved. But then when we try to evangelize we make it sound like they have to live a perfect life in order to be saved. We know that salvation is by faith and not by works, but we treat others as if they are not saved because they sin. Shame on us! We look down on people that God accepts, and blaspheme the gospel by implying that sinners cannot be saved, showing hate and implying that we are more worthy than them to receive God's grace. Shame on us!

We should remember that we ourselves are no better in God's eyes than they are because we are nothing but sinners ourselves and we still sin even when we try so hard not to. Even if we try to cover it up, we must remember that we cannot get rid of our sin nature. We must realize that even though we think we cover it so well, it is still there in our core and God sees it easily. Covering it up does not get rid of it. That is why Jesus said that others would know a true disciple of Jesus because he will have love for others. We need to learn to be much more accepting of sinners. Christians can sin as much as they want and still be saved, but they will always have remorse because they know they are doing wrong. So Christians can sin, but they cannot really like it. We must remember that our job is only to remind people of sin. It is the Holy Spirit's job to turn them from it. We need to learn that our job is to show love and to evangelize. Judging and making people righteous is God's job. We have not been given and will never be given the right to do God's job.

First Corinthians 13 says, "Love is patient, love is kind, love does not envy, is not boastful, is not conceited, does not act improperly, is not selfish, is not provoked, does not keep a record of wrongs…" If you are judging others, then you are not acting according to this description, which means that you are not showing love and are therefore acting contrary to the gospel. Do not judge!

How does "be holy because you know it's the right thing to do" and "accept people who are not holy" fit into the same religion when they seem to be opposite and mutually exclusive? It's like this: be holy because you know it's the right thing to do, but even though you try so hard, you still cannot get rid of your sin nature. Even though you try so hard to be righteous, you are still only a sinner and always will be, so you must accept people who are not holy because you must recognize that you yourself are not holy even when you try your hardest. Also, if God accepts people as they are and forgives them, then why can't you? Why would a holy God keep loving and forgiving people who just keep turning away? Why indeed! Why did we ever deserve God's love? We didn't! Halellujah!

P.S. I realize that in this chapter I have been talking to people who look down on sinners, and I may have implied that sin is okay, but as a word to those who think that sin is okay and would use this chapter to justify it, remember that in order to be saved you first have to admit that sin is wrong. It is this realization that sin is wrong and your love for God that are supposed to make you want to turn from sin. Those who judge sinners have no right to judge, but they do have God's commission to call your attention to right and wrong. Remember that the point of salvation is *fellowship* with God.

Basics of the Faith

Jesus's Divinity

Old Testament messianic prophesies, Jesus, and the New Testament clearly teach that Jesus is divine, that He is God. But it is not that Jesus only has some of the nature of God. He has all the nature of God. He is fully God and fully man. In fact, the meaning of the name Immanuel is "God with us." This means that Jesus is God in the flesh. Jesus is God, who took on human physiology and nature and came down to our level and spoke to us in a language we could understand so that He could show His love for us even though we were only sinners and to show us His desire to save us from our sins because of His great love. It is clear that the Jews of Jesus's day understood this because in the gospels there are accounts of the Jews trying to stone Jesus when He claimed to be the Son of God. Stoning was the punishment for someone claiming to be God. Also, if you read the gospels, you will find many passages where Jesus tells His disciples that He was with God from the beginning or that He and God are one.

The Trinity

God, Jesus, and the Holy Spirit are one. They are not three different gods. They are the same God. We must not consider them separate. Whenever we think of God, we must think of Him as the Trinity. No one part of the Trinity is any more important than the others. I have heard of some people who say that they like to think about one of the three and not about the others. This is a mistake! We must consider them all three as one. In fact, it is an official heresy of the Christian church to say that they are separate. In the early centuries of the Christian church, a man named Arius came up with the concept that God, Jesus, and the Holy Spirit were three separate beings made of the same substance. He taught that the Son was created by the Father. This is called the Arian heresy. The Bible teaches that the Trinity is not just three gods made of the same substance but is actually one God. They are not similar; they are the same. Official church doctrine says that the Trinity is one and that they are inseparable. This is what is taught throughout the New Testament.

The Two Covenants

In the Old Testament, God made His covenant with the Jews. It said that if the people keep His commands He will be their God and they will be His people. But as you read the Old Testament, you see that the people always end up backsliding into a life of sinfulness. Thus, the old covenant falls short not because of God, but because of the people. God knew from the beginning that this covenant was not sufficient. He knew that the people would mess it up. But the reason He made this covenant was that He wanted to show us that we could not live up to it. He had to show us why He was going to make the new covenant. The new covenant is that all who believe in Jesus will have eternal life. In order to believe that Jesus paid for your sins, you must admit that you are nothing but a vile sinner who cannot earn his own way to heaven. Those who believe in the old covenant put themselves on a pedestal equal with God by implying that they can be good enough for God. But those who believe in the new covenant put God on a pedestal far above themselves by implying that they can never be good enough for God by believing that it is simply God's grace that saves them.

Those who believe in the old covenant also put themselves on a pedestal above other people by implying that if they go to heaven because they are good and others go to hell because they are bad, then they must be better than other people. But those who believe in the new covenant place themselves on equal footing with all other people by implying that everybody is sinful and that we all need a Savior. The new covenant is better than the old covenant because it puts all men on the same level and puts God on a pedestal far above them. It also is better because it doesn't rely on our works (which we have proven that we cannot get right) but on our faith (which is the only thing we can get right). The Old Testament says that man is sinful and is incapable of attaining salvation on his own, that something else can die to pay the penalty for our sin for us (the sacrifice system), and that man has to have enough sacrifice to pay for each of his many sins, and the Old Testament promises one who will pay for all our sins. The New Testament says that Jesus is enough to pay for the sins of the whole world, that the way we take part in that sacrifice is simply through faith, and that no one can attain salvation except through Jesus because they cannot make enough sacrifices. Thus, for someone who does not accept Jesus, the Old Testament says that he is too sinful, that he did not offer enough sacrifice to pay for his sins, and that he failed to see the symbolism of the sacrifice system and also failed to study the prophesies of who the Messiah is and what He will do for us, and the New Testament agrees so there are two witnesses against him. But for someone who does believe in Jesus, the Old Testament says that he must have enough sacrifice to pay for his sins, but the New Testament says that he has the sacrifice provided by God and foreshadowed in the Old Testament that will pay for all his sins. So there are two witnesses against someone who doesn't believe in Jesus and two witnesses for someone who does believe in Jesus.

Resurrection

Resurrection is an essential belief in Christianity. Look at 1 Corinthians 15. Since this chapter sums up better than I can why resurrection is essential to Christianity, I won't try to explain it. As you read, notice that resurrection is essential because we believe that Jesus was raised from the dead, that Jesus's resurrection proves that we will be resurrected, that baptism is based on resurrection, that our resurrection body will be sinless, and that the victory of righteousness lies not in ourselves but in God and our resurrection at the end times.

Praying in Jesus's Name

This is a simple concept that most people don't understand. It's not just saying "in Jesus's name" at the end of a prayer. A person cannot come directly to God and ask for anything because he is sinful. Man always needs an intercessor. But since Jesus already paid for our sins, we have the right to go directly to God and ask for anything. We do not pray to Jesus (or especially to the saints) to intercede for us because we do not need an intercessor. So what it means to pray in Jesus's name is to go directly to God and ask what we will because we have that right through Jesus. We can go directly to God at any time and ask for anything without an intercessor because Jesus has given us His perfect righteousness. Basically, praying in Jesus's name is praying with the righteousness that He has given us.

Witnessing Is the Goal

Our ultimate goal as Christians is to become fishers of men, to spread the gospel. This can be done aggressively or passively. Aggressive evangelism is walking up to somebody and telling them that Jesus died for their sins. It's usually not easy, but it can be effective. Passive evangelism is simply asking someone if they go to church, if they would like to go to church with you, if they believe in God, or if you can pray for them about anything. It's easy because the person will lead you to their spiritual needs and there is no pressure. The conversation may lead to a decision to accept Jesus as their Savior, or it may simply be the first time the person has thought about whether they really believe in God. You ask a simple question and then meet the spiritual needs that they reveal. My Sunday school teacher calls this the salvation line: is there a God—going to church—soul searching—salvation—living for Christ. There are usually many people along someone's salvation line. Each one has only a small job. This may be because God wants us to be well rounded by coming into contact with many different types of Christians. If all you do is to get the person thinking about if they believe in God, then pat yourself on the back because you have started them on the path of finding God since they will always be searching for God. Now they will always be open to talking about spiritual things. Also remember that you cannot witness by your lifestyle. People will either just see you as a good person or will be turned away because they think they have to be good, which they know they can't. You must be vocal about your belief that you are no better than any other person and about your gratefulness to God for His grace.

Baptism

Baptism is seen by many people as the point where we are saved. This is wrong. Baptism is not required for salvation. It is merely our public proclamation that we are already saved. John's baptism and Jesus's baptism are different. John's baptism is about admitting you are a sinner and repenting. It is symbolic of your death to your old ways and your commitment to a righteous life. It is a works baptism that is based solely on you. To believe in John's baptism is to believe that salvation is all about being good. In order for this to work, you would have to be perfect, which would mean you don't need Jesus. John's baptism falls short because it relies on us. We can never be good enough for God. The only reason John baptized is to get people to admit that they are sinners. But John's baptism never took any sins away. If all you see in baptism is John's baptism, then you probably don't have a clear concept of the new covenant. Jesus's baptism is a symbol of many things: 1) Your faith that Jesus died and was raised from the dead; 2) Your faith that Jesus is all you need because He paid your sin debt for you; 3) Your faith that you have a new spiritual life through Jesus (born again: John 1:12-13); 4) Your death to a life of slavery to the law and your new life of love that reflects the gospel; 5) Since baptism takes place in water and we are totally immersed, it represents that Jesus has fully cleansed us; 6) Since baptism is done in the name of the Father, Son, and Holy Spirit, it symbolizes that through the Son you have direct access to the Father and fellowship with Him through the Holy Spirit.

Jesus's baptism is based solely on your faith in Jesus, not in anything you do. John's baptism is inadequate for the same reason the old covenant is inadequate: they rely on us. Jesus's baptism is adequate for the same reason the new covenant is adequate: they rely on your belief that Jesus is all you need. I say adequate, but what I really mean is exceeding abundant. The new covenant and Jesus's baptism rely on the only thing man is capable of getting right: faith.

Why Sunday?

The Sabbath is the last day of the week, which is Saturday. So why do we go to church on Sunday? The reason is that we want to celebrate the fact that Jesus rose from the dead on Sunday. Also, Sunday is the first day of the workweek, and we need to remember that Jesus has given us a new job to do: loving, giving, forgiving, and witnessing that all reflect the gospel.

Additional Thoughts

Imagine the ultimate football game. The sta-dium is enormous, the field is huge, and the rules are that anyone can jump in and play at any time. On one team are God, the angels, and Christians, and on the other team are the demons and the world. You don't have to be a minister to be on mission for God. You can be on mission for God in your workplace and among your friends. After all, since they don't go to church, you may be the only one who can share the gospel with them. We must realize that the world is full of people who are either lost or have gotten away from God. We need to be on the lookout for them so that we can bring them back. They will not come to God on their own, and they will not come to church on their own in order for the preacher to reach them. Their only hope is us! Since anyone can play any position at any time, you can either be in the bleachers, on the sideline, or on the field in any position. What do you want to do? What play can you make for God?

Which of the following is our source of theology: pastor, seminary, denomination, or elders? The answer is none! These all represent the wisdom of man. The Bible is our one true source of theology because it is the Word of God. The wisdom of God always trumps the wisdom of man. If any of the previous disagrees in the slightest way with the Bible, it is wrong. Also look out for correct biblical interpretation. Often someone will quote one verse (or even part of a verse) by itself and give their interpretation. Then when you go back and read the whole text you see that it is actually talking about something else. Never read a verse by itself. Always read it in context. Context is *everything* in biblical interpretation!

The symbols of Christianity tell us a lot about the true nature of our religion. Let's look at the cross first. It tells us that the main aspect of Christianity is that Jesus died to pay the price for our sins. It is also a bare cross, which means that He rose from the dead and this guarantees our place in heaven. Our main focus should not be on our own righteousness since Jesus already has that covered. Our righteousness is merely a secondary (but important) consideration. Jesus didn't come to make us be more righteous. He came to give us His own righteousness. Jesus being the only way to heaven is the biggest thing that separates Christianity from any other religion. The gospel *is* our religion. If the gospel is our religion, then the gospel should be the main focus of our religion. Now let's look at the fish. When Jesus gathered His disciples, He said, "Follow Me and I will make you *fishers of men.*" The real focus of Christianity is fishing for lost souls. If the gospel is our religion, then church should be about equipping us for evangelism, not just righteousness. Preachers should be asking us how many people we told about Jesus, not just how good we've been.

One of the things I have seen in my personal Bible study is that when Jesus heals someone, He says that it is their faith that heals them. Also, when someone comes to Jesus to be healed, many times He almost ignores their request for physical healing and goes straight to saying "your sins have been forgiven." This means that Jesus sees their physical needs as temporary and easy to bear in relation to their spiritual needs. In other words, it's better to live a life of physical torment yet receive forgiveness of sins than to live a life of perfect health and go to hell. Jesus always addresses the most urgent needs first. Also it is the person's faith that allows them to be healed and made whole just as it is our faith in Christ's death and resurrection that allows us to receive forgiveness of sins and be made spiritually perfect in God's eyes. In some of Jesus's healing stories, the only reason He healed the person is to show the people that He has the power to forgive sins. Anyone can say that a person is forgiven of sins, but that doesn't necessarily mean it's true. Jesus proves His authority to forgive sins by healing the person. Thus, Jesus's ability to heal physical sickness proves His authority to heal spiritually, to forgive sins. Also look at Hebrews 11. It is clear that God has always blessed and will always bless based on faith.

What is our goal as Christians? To become fishers of men! This means that our main priority and our goal in life is to fulfill the Great Commission: witnessing and making disciples. It's not enough to be charitable and uphold the law. These two are good things, and they reflect the gospel, but our focus is to *spread* the gospel. In John 20:23, Jesus says to the disciples, "If you forgive the sins of any, they are forgiven them; if you retain the sins of any, they are retained." Since it is up to the new believer to believe and thereby receive forgiveness of sins, Jesus is giving the disciples the authority to give out forgiveness of sins to all who will accept it. But if we do not spread the gospel, the people will not hear and thus will not receive forgiveness of sins. We can spread the gospel and take others to heaven with us, or we can be silent and be responsible for letting them go to hell. Read Romans 15:14-21. In this passage, Paul is clearly more concerned with evangelism than building up of righteousness. Second Timothy 4:1-5 says,

> Before God and Christ Jesus, who is going to judge the living and the dead, and by His appearing and His kingdom, I solemnly charge you: proclaim the message; persist in it whether convenient or not; rebuke, correct, and encourage with great courage and teaching. For the time will come when they will not tolerate sound doctrine, but according to their own desires, will accumulate teachers for themselves because they have an itch to hear something new. They will turn away from hearing the truth and will turn aside to myths. But as for you, keep a clear head about everything, endure hardship, do the work of an evangelist, fulfill your ministry.

Be sure that the people you evangelize learn correct doctrine, become spiritually mature in sound doctrine, and turn out to be evangelists.

We must remember that all our denominations are the same church, the Christian church, Christ's church. We must also remember that each of our denominations is imperfect because each has customs that are from the wisdom of man and not the Word of God. We must also remember that in every church, there are members who are not saved because they have either not grasped the concept that Jesus has already paid for our sins or they simply don't truly believe. They are just going along with the motions. Just as no man is any better than any other man, so no church is any better than another. So we must all love and respect our fellow churches, and we must all work together because we are all really trying to do the same thing: save souls. In John 10:16, Jesus says, "But I have other sheep that are not of this fold; I must bring them also, and they will listen to my voice. Then there will be one flock, one shepherd." Jesus prays,

> May they all become one, as You, Father, are in Me and I am in You. May they also be one in Us, so that the world may believe You sent Me. May they be one as We are one. I am in them and you are in Me. May they be made completely one, so the world may know You have sent Me and have loved them as you have loved Me.

> John 17:21-23

Also read 1 Corinthians 1:10-17, Ephesians 4:4-6, and Philippians 2:1-4. It's clear that we are all on the same team. If we cannot work together, then we should obviously take some time and figure out where our priorities are: on the gospel or on smaller theological squabbling.

One question I want to address is "what makes a person saved?" Some people think they are saved because they said the sinner's prayer and got baptized. That's not true. As you read the New Testament, it becomes clear that salvation is purely through faith, not by anything the person does. I want to clarify the prayer and baptism for you. If all the salvation verses in the New Testament say that a person is saved purely through faith (which they do), then why say the sinner's prayer? It's simply because most people feel like they need to pray anyway. Also look at Mark 10:46-52. Here we see that Jesus ignores the man's first plea for help because it is so general. It is only after the man specifically tells Jesus what he wants that he gets his sight. I know that I am saved only through faith, but when I see this passage, it makes me want to tell God exactly what I believe for two reasons. First, it helps me because I can express my belief in a sentence or two and clarify it for myself. Second, I know that God knows exactly what I believe about why I am saved. I believe that our invitations in our churches and our calling for decisions in personal evangelism should only be about recognizing that you have sinned and believing that Jesus paid your debt for you because this is what saves you. Turning from your sins and making Jesus Lord of your life should not be part of our invitations or calling for decisions because they do not save us. They are not even part of our salvation. They are part of our growth after salvation. Also, baptism has nothing to do with salvation. It is merely our way of showing publicly that we believe Jesus died to pay the price for our sins and rose again on the third day and thus is our way of publicly proclaiming that we are already saved.

Conclusion

So what's the point? Ephesians 2:8-10 says,

> For by grace you are saved through faith, and this is
> not from yourselves; it is God's gift- not from works so
> that no man can boast. For we are His creation- cre-
> ated is Christ Jesus for good works, which God pre-
> pared ahead of time so that we should walk in them.

Romans 7:13-25 also says that we will still sin but that we
should have an internal struggle between desires for sin and
desires for godliness. Paul is saying that we cannot earn or
keep our salvation through works. But 2 Peter 2 seems to
say that we can lose our salvation by continuing in sin. The
reason there is a seeming contradiction is that 2 Peter 2 is
misunderstood. It is not saying that those who continue in
sin are not saved; it is saying that those who believe that sin
is not bad cannot be saved. First John 1:8-10 says,

> If we say, "We have no sin," we are deceiving our-
> selves, and the truth is not in us. If we confess our
> sins, He is faithful and righteous to forgive us our sins
> and to cleanse us from all unrighteousness. If we say,
> "We have not sinned," we make Him a liar and His
> word is not in us.

Jesus cannot die for sins that are not wrong, so you cannot be saved if you do not first admit that you are a sinner and that sin is wrong. Therefore, those who teach that sin is okay are not saved because they don't truly believe that Jesus died for their sins since Jesus cannot die for what is not wrong. That is why in order to be saved we must admit that sin is wrong, and we must have at least some desire to do right. Salvation is through faith alone, but you can only have faith in Jesus if you believe that you are a sinner and know that sin is wrong.

We don't have to keep the law in order to maintain salvation. We are saved no matter what we do, but that does not mean that God is pleased with us. We should want to obey God even though we know we don't have to just because we know that's what's right. Loving, forgiving, charity, and witnessing are commands that we have been given because they reflect the gospel, and it is always within our power to do them. We should always keep these commands and never forsake them because to forsake them is to live contrary to the gospel. In fact, we should look for opportunities to display them. Our righteousness is simply out of love for God.

Everybody is different. This is good because everybody in the world is different, and it takes different kinds of people to reach them. Someone who is "goody-goody" cannot reach the kinds of people who say "I'm not ready to be that good" and someone who is sinning cannot reach the people who try to uphold the law. God has given some of us the ability to be righteous and let others of us struggle, but it is not that He favors some of us over others; it's so that we can reach the world. But we can all show love, charity, forgiveness, and share the gospel at all times. This is the mission God has given us. Everybody naturally falls into certain categories of spiritual gifts. Some are givers, some are servers, some are worshipful, some are theological, some are good at not sinning, some can't stop sinning, some are patient, some are strict, etc... But we should all be friends with opposite types because we can learn from them and they can learn from us. Although everybody naturally has only one or two gifts, our life goal as a Christian is to be able to do all of them well as needed. We should yearn for the life goal of being well balanced—not just in our knowledge but in our exercise of that knowledge.

Look at Ephesians 2:10. What are the "good works" that we are created for? They are loving, giving, forgiving, repentance, and witnessing that reflect the gospel. Always be as concerned about loving, giving, forgiving, and sharing the gospel as about your righteousness. Our goal is not to only focus on our own righteousness; it's also to focus on loving, giving, forgiving, and becoming fishers of men. God has already taken care of our righteousness. Since God has taken care of us, we shouldn't put our focus only on ourselves. That would mean that all our focus is on what's already taken care of and our faith in Jesus is weak. Our focus is supposed to be on what's not already taken care of: other people's needs and salvation. God has taken care of you. Who have you taken care of? As a Christian, your life is not about you; it's about others. Remember John 3:16. God loves, gives, forgives, accepts. Show it and share it.

Anybody can love, give, forgive, witness, and at least recognize their need to do right, but only a select few can even begin to understand how to live a godly life or how to let God live through you. The reason most people can't live a godly life is that the method for denying sin is not part of our human nature. But this doesn't mean that it is okay to live in sin just because it is part of your nature and you don't know how to stop. Sin is still bad. God still doesn't like it even though He has paid for it by giving His Son in our place. It's just that the secret to godly living is hidden in the Bible and is not easy to do. But that doesn't mean we should ignore it. Instead, we should be *searching* for it. It's like Jeremiah 33:3 says: "Call to Me and I will answer you and show you great and wondrous things you do not know." But that's just the thing; we have to call unto Him and ask Him to reveal it to us. We cannot find it on our own, but if we search the Scriptures, God will show it to us and it will blow our minds! If we just ask, He'll just give it to us! Keep searching!

I wish I could go into detail and let you in on all the secrets. But the truth is that I haven't yet had time to truly search the Scriptures and find the secrets. I'm still a relatively new Christian and am still struggling with my sin myself. But I hope that one day I will be able to unlock all the secrets to godly living and share them with you. Until then, good luck in your Christian life.

I think everybody should study apologetics. Apologetics is basically just defending your faith logically to skeptics. For the scientifically minded, evolution does not stand up to science as well as creation, and geology actually supports the flood of Genesis. All the messianic prophecies of the Old Testament really do point to Jesus (and there are plenty of them). And for those who want to witness to people of other religions or cultures, there are books to help you. You should be able to find these things in any good Christian book store. I highly recommend it.

Don't confuse your service for God and your relationship with Him. It is your relationship that produces your service, not the other way around. The whole point of the Christian life is really about *choosing* to live for God.